FOOD in a GLOBAL VILLAGE

GARY MILLER

ISBN: 978-1-63813-379-7

Cover and interior design: Kristi Yoder

Image credits:
Christian Aid Ministries photos: pages 4, 8, 9, 17, 23, 33, 38 , 54, 60, 62, 63, 66, 74, 75, 101, 105, 113, 128, 137, 149, 156, 158, 164–165, back cover
Christian Aid Ministries artwork: page155, Gloria Oostema
Page 18: https://www.ensisfisheries.com/frozen-yellowfin-tuna-eye/
Page 21: https://commons.wikimedia.org/wiki/File:Balut001.jpg
Page 40: https://www.wonderslist.com/10-weird-foods-eaten-around-the-world/
Adobe Stock photos: pages 11, 13, 14, 20, 24, 26, 29, 30, 34, 38, , 42, 47, 49, 51, 53, 59, 65, 69, 77, 82, 88, 94, 96, 107, 109, 111, 126, 130, 133, 135, 142, 145, 147
Shutterstock photos: pages 37, 86

Printed in Hong Kong

Published by:

CAM Books
P.O. Box 355
Berlin, Ohio 44610 USA
Phone: 330.893.4828
Fax: 330.893.4893
cambooks.org

Contents

Everyone I have ever met likes good food. Yet we don't live very long or travel very far until we discover that people around the world describe "good food" quite differently. There is a great difference not only in what we eat but also in how much we consume.

To get a better picture of global reality, let's shrink the world down to a village of 100 people.

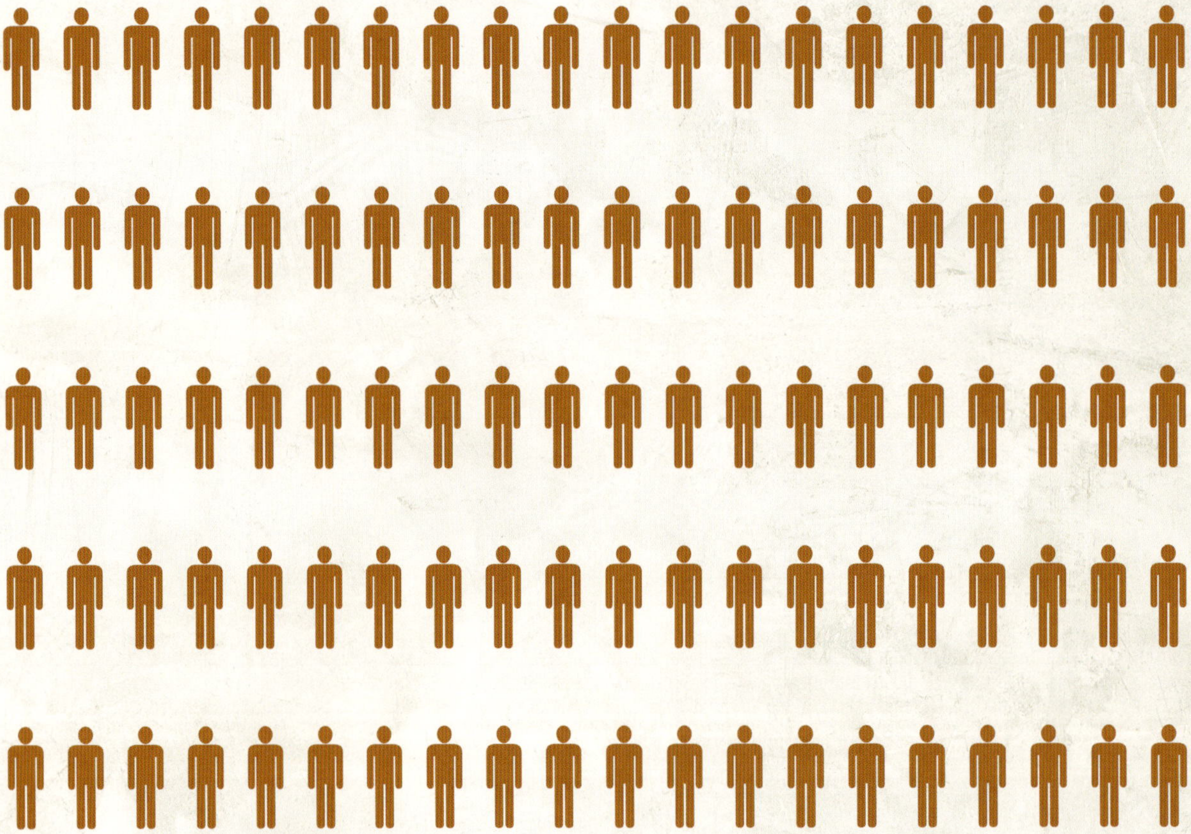

If the World Were
a Village of 100

Each of the stick figures represents a little
over 80 million people. So if you lived
in a global village of 100 people, what
kinds of food would the villagers eat? What
smells might be wafting down the street?

18

Eighteen of your neighbors would be from India, so when you open your door, there might be a strong smell of curry drifting down the street.

And your next-door neighbors might be
having tandoori chicken with chapatis.

India

China

18

Eighteen neighbors would be from China, and they would be enjoying a very different diet.

They might be eating noodles, rice, or
chopped vegetables. If you stopped in,
they might offer you pork or fried duck.

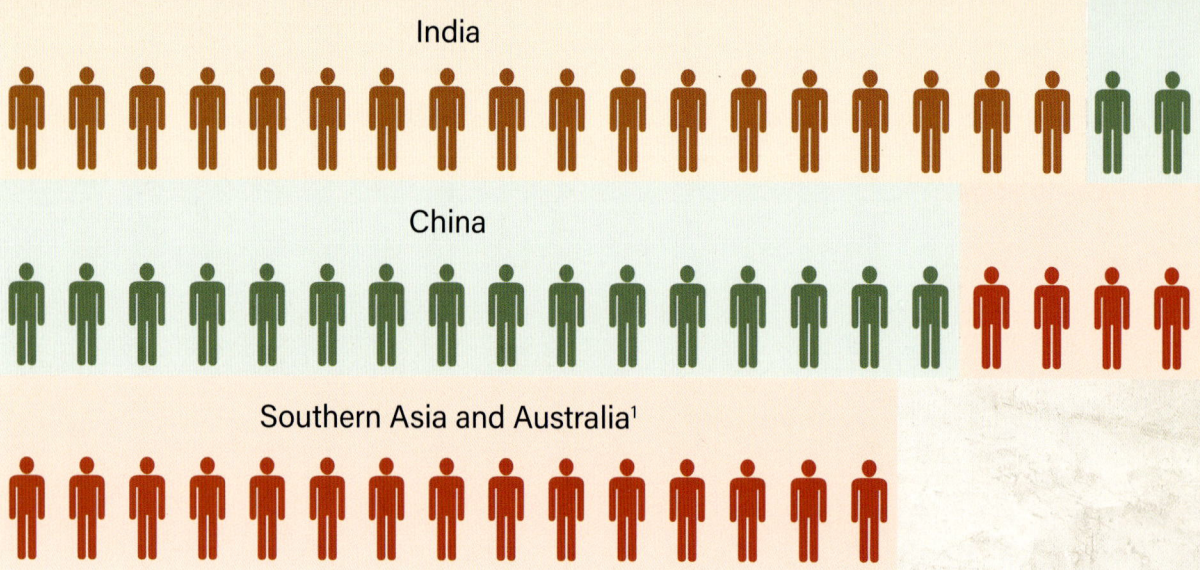

India

China

Southern Asia and Australia[1]

[1] Australia is not mentioned in the text because of its relatively low population. Less than half a person would be from Australia.

19

Nineteen in your village would be from the rest of Asia—from countries like Thailand, Malaysia, Vietnam, and Japan. The diet in these homes would be similar to that of the Chinese, and you might find some unusual foods you have difficulty classifying as "good."

Your Japanese neighbors might be enjoying
tuna eyeballs, boiled and served with
a light soy sauce. This is a dish many
from Japan consider extremely tasty!

You might find
your Cambodian
friends eating
fried spiders.
The spiders are
marinated in
sugar and salt and
fried in garlic.

Your Filipino neighbors might tell you of a favorite delicacy from their country—duck embryo that has been boiled alive in its shell.

Known as balut, this might seem like a strange dish to you, but it is sold by street vendors in the Philippines.

India

China

Southern Asia and Australia

Africa

22

Twenty-two homes in your
village would be from the
various countries in Africa.

If you stopped in you might be served fufu, a doughy food made from cassava. It is eaten with a spicy soup and often accompanied by whatever meat is available. Fufu is so smooth and stretchy that it can be swallowed without chewing!

Or you might find an African family sitting
around enjoying their evening munching on
fried grasshoppers. They are delicious when
seasoned with salt, pepper, and other spices.
 You would find them similar to popcorn—
except that sometimes a little juice
squirts out when you bite into one.

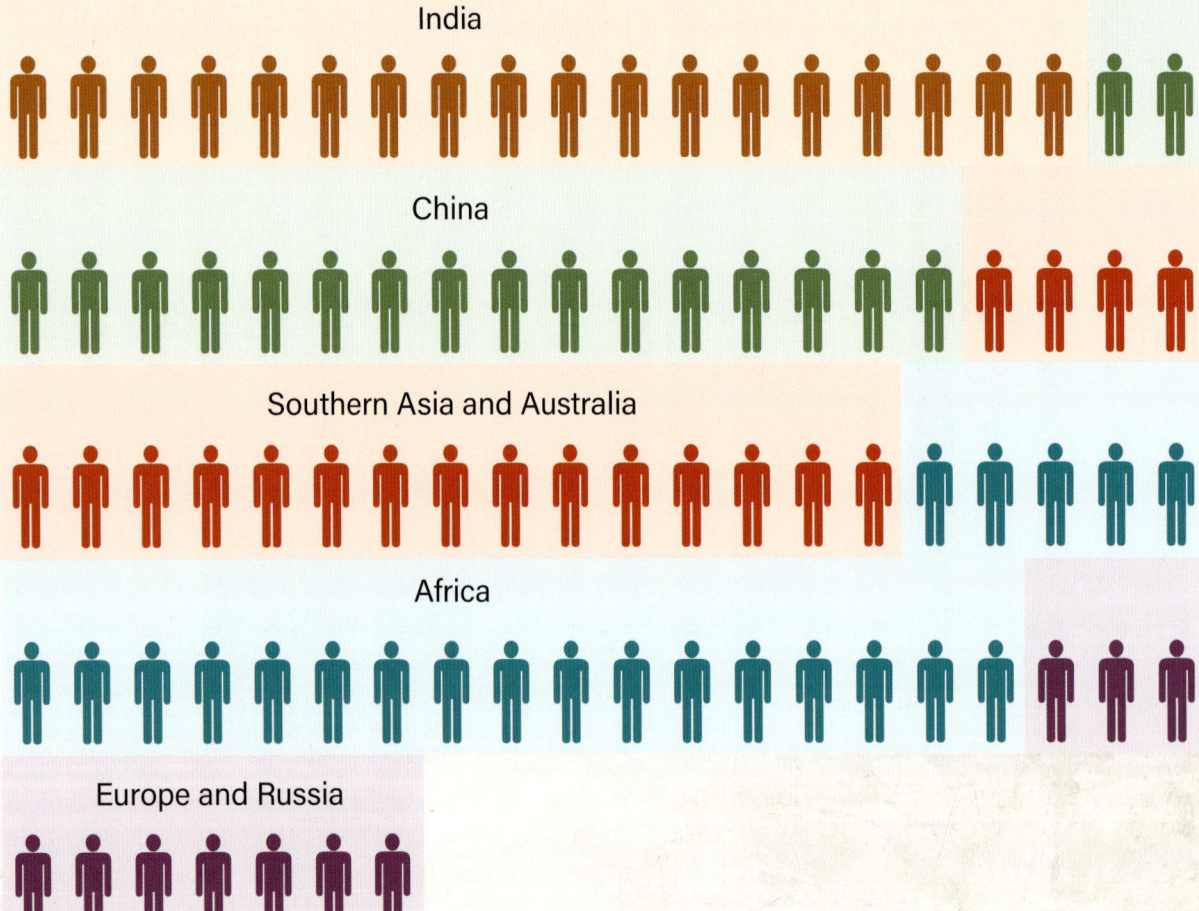

India

China

Southern Asia and Australia

Africa

Europe and Russia

10

Ten in your village would be from Europe
or Russia. You might find a wealthy
French neighbor eating escargot, a snail
delicacy, while your Italian neighbor
is sitting down to some kind of pasta.

Your Ukrainian neighbors would probably be eating salo, similar to raw bacon, with their borscht.

The first time I was served salo, I was both apprehensive and curious. "Won't eating raw pork make me sick?" I asked.

My host laughed and said, "It only makes you sick in America!"

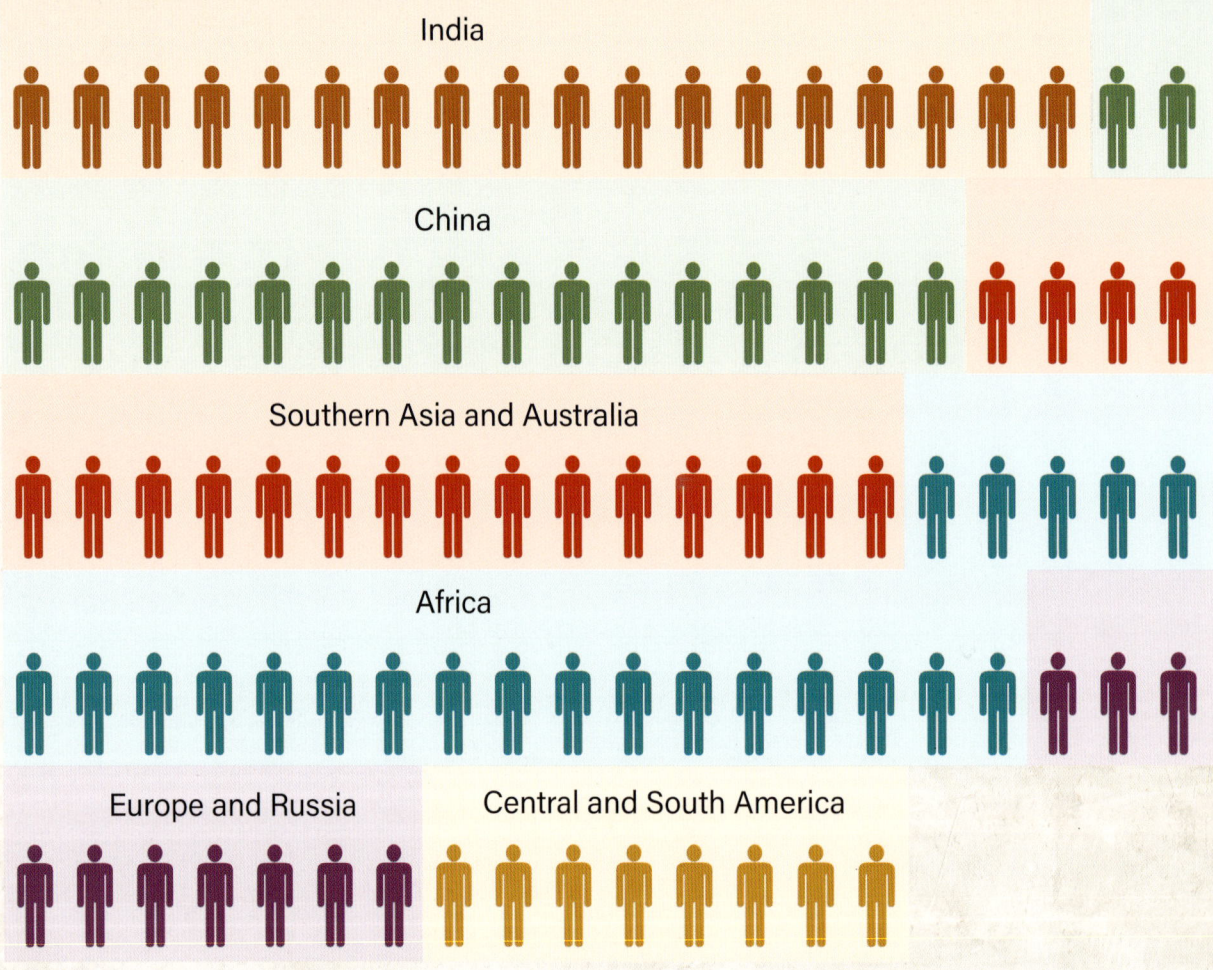

India

China

Southern Asia and Australia

Africa

Europe and Russia

Central and South America

8

Eight villagers would be from Central and South America. They would, of course, serve lots of beans and tortillas. But they also enjoy many other foods.

Your El Salvadoran friend might serve you
tasty pupusas, which are like tortillas
stuffed with cheese, beans, or meat.
 Or you might find villagers from the high
plateaus of Peru eating various kinds
of potatoes.

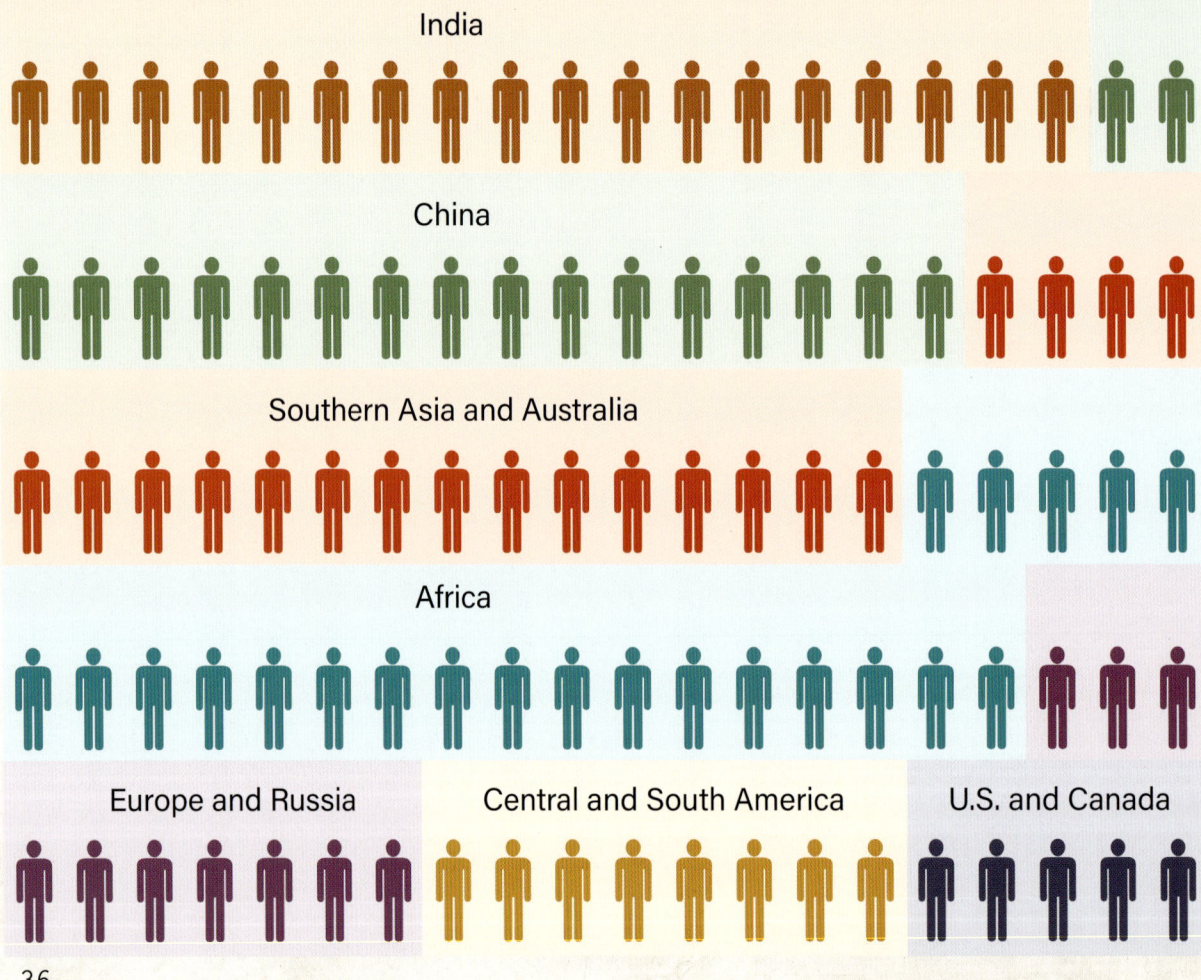

India

China

Southern Asia and Australia

Africa

Europe and Russia

Central and South America

U.S. and Canada

5

Finally, five villagers would hail from the United States and Canada. The diet of these American and Canadian friends might seem quite bland compared to the rest of the village.
 You would probably find a family eating fried chicken or some kind of barbecued meat.

At least one of the households would probably be having hamburgers. The average American consumes over 150 hamburgers each year, or 3 per week. Considering the fact that some Americans don't like burgers, someone is eating a lot of hamburgers!

Yet, even in America, if you poke around a little, you will find people eating some strange foods.

In Alaska, Eskimos still eat stinkheads.
This is a traditional food of the Inuit
people who live in southwestern Alaska.
In the past, stinkheads were prepared
by placing salmon heads and innards in a
wooden barrel, then covering them with
burlap and burying everything in the
ground for about a week. Today, plastic
bags and buckets have replaced the wooden
barrel, but the outcome is the same. It is
described as a fermented putty-like mush.

Or you might visit a local grocery store
and come across another strange food.

SPAM is a brand of salty canned pork. It was introduced in 1937 and gained popularity after being used by Allied troops during World War II.

In the United States, Hawaii has the highest per capita consumption of SPAM. Because of its high fat and sodium content, it has never been promoted as a health food. Sales of SPAM tend to increase during American economic downturns.

How Your Neighbors
Eat Their Food

Obviously, there would be a wide array of foods
being consumed in your village! As you visit
your neighbors' homes, you would encounter
a wide variety of smells and flavors.
And not only would the food your
neighbors consume be different, so
would be the way they eat it.

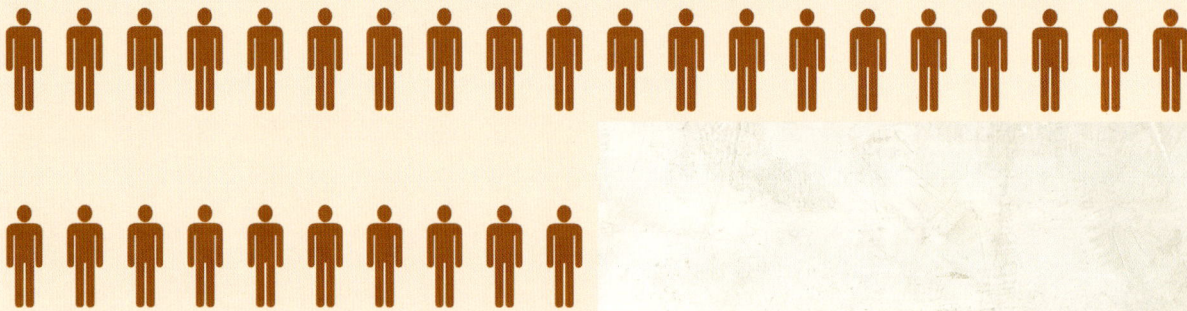

Eat with hands—no utensils

30

Thirty of the homes would not use any utensils at mealtime. They would simply eat with their hands.

Eat with hands—no utensils

Use chopsticks

22

Twenty-two of your neighbors
would eat with chopsticks.

Eat with hands—no utensils

Use chopsticks

Use fork and spoon

48

The remaining 48 would eat their meals primarily with a fork and spoon.
  What about sitting positions while eating?

Sit on the floor to eat

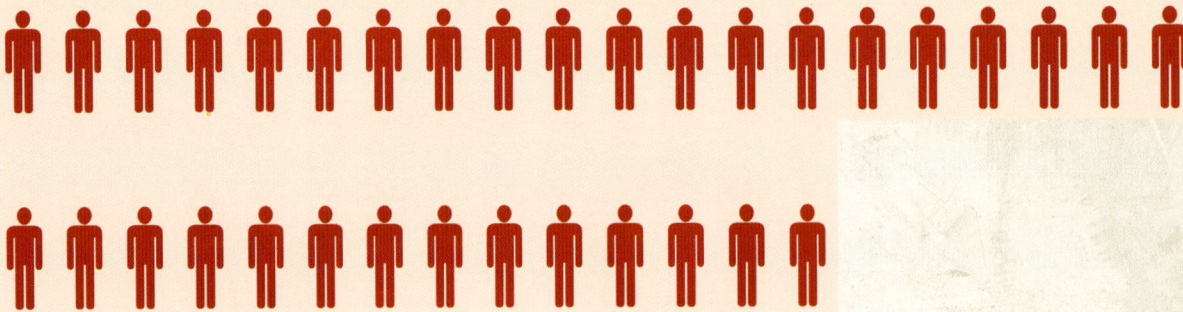

Sitting Positions
While Eating

About a third of the people in your village would eat their meals while sitting on the floor.

Many believe eating on the floor is more comfortable. It allows them to sit cross-legged or in other traditional positions. Others believe sitting on the floor during meals is more respectful and is a better way to connect with others. Some even believe eating on the floor improves digestion.

Sit on the floor to eat

Eat at a table

But the other two-thirds disagree. They grew up using a table and chairs and see eating on the floor as uncomfortable and even unsanitary. How we are raised has a huge impact on our perspective on issues like this.

What about kitchen appliances? How would your neighbors cook their food?

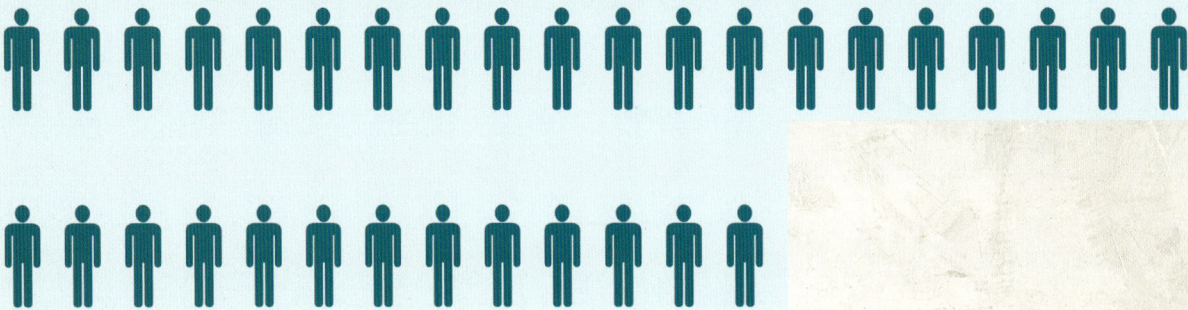

Cook by building a fire with wood, coal, animal dung, etc.

How the Village Cooks Its Food

Thirty-three households would cook with firewood, charcoal, coal, animal dung, or various types of crop waste. As a result, smoke would seep out of many homes, adding to the mixture of unusual smells on the street.

The inside of your Indian neighbor's
kitchen might look something like
this. Simple stoves made of clay
are very common in southern Asia.

You would find your neighbors from
Africa and countries like Haiti
cooking directly over an open fire.

All they need is a few rocks, a pot, and some
fuel to start cooking a delicious meal.

Cook by building a fire with wood, coal, animal dung, etc.

Cook with gas or electricity

67

The remaining 67 more affluent neighbors would cook with electricity or some kind of gas. This is much cleaner and safer than using an open fire.

What about other kitchen appliances?

Homes with no refrigerator

Homes Without
Refrigerators

Twenty-three families would not have a refrigerator in their home. Many of them would simply walk down to the local store to purchase the food they need each day. Many countries have small stores within walking distance, so people keep very little food in their homes.

Homes with no refrigerator

Homes with a refrigerator

77

The other 77 homes would have some kind of refrigerator—and a few very wealthy neighbors would even have more than one.

You would also discover that refrigerators in your village vary greatly in size, with the largest ones in American and Canadian homes.

An even greater disparity would be in how many homes have their own freezer.

Homes with no freezer

Homes with a freezer

90

Ninety homes would not have a freezer. Having a personal freezer would be a luxury in this village, with only **ten homes** having their own.

10

While homes around the world differ in kinds of food, everyone has to eat, as we all need energy to survive.So let's take a closer look at what foods in your village supply this energy.

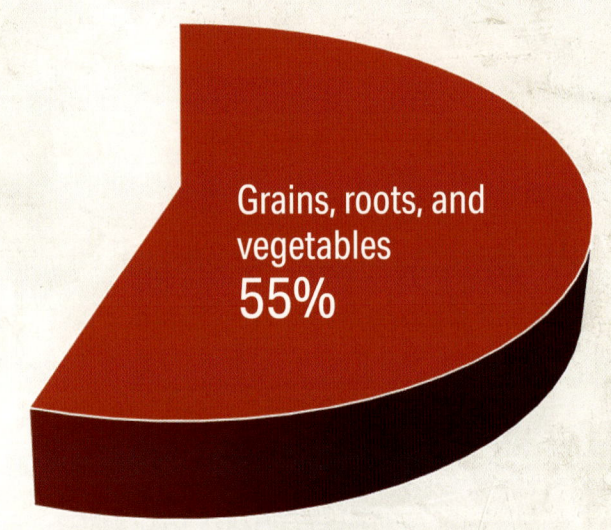

Grains, roots, and vegetables
55%

Where Would the Village's Calories Come From?

The majority of all the calories
in your village, 55%, would come
directly from things farmers grow.
Grains, roots, and vegetables are
a staple for much of the world.

This means you would probably see people selling all kinds of grains and vegetables along the road, like this lady in South Sudan.

Seventeen percent of the calories would come from meat, eggs, and dairy.

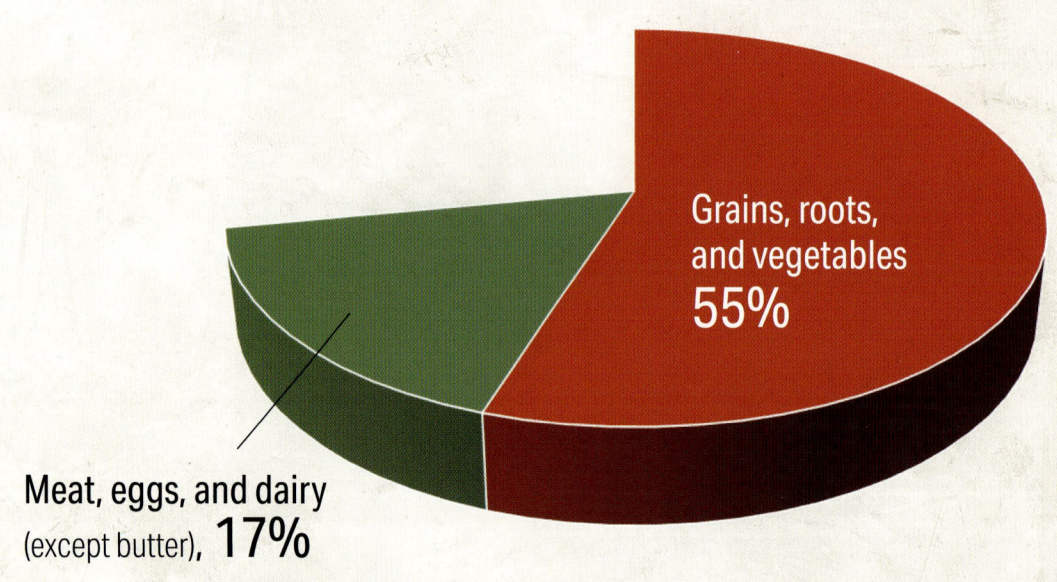

Grains, roots, and vegetables
55%

Meat, eggs, and dairy
(except butter), 17%

These are the more expensive products, so they would primarily be found in the wealthiest homes.

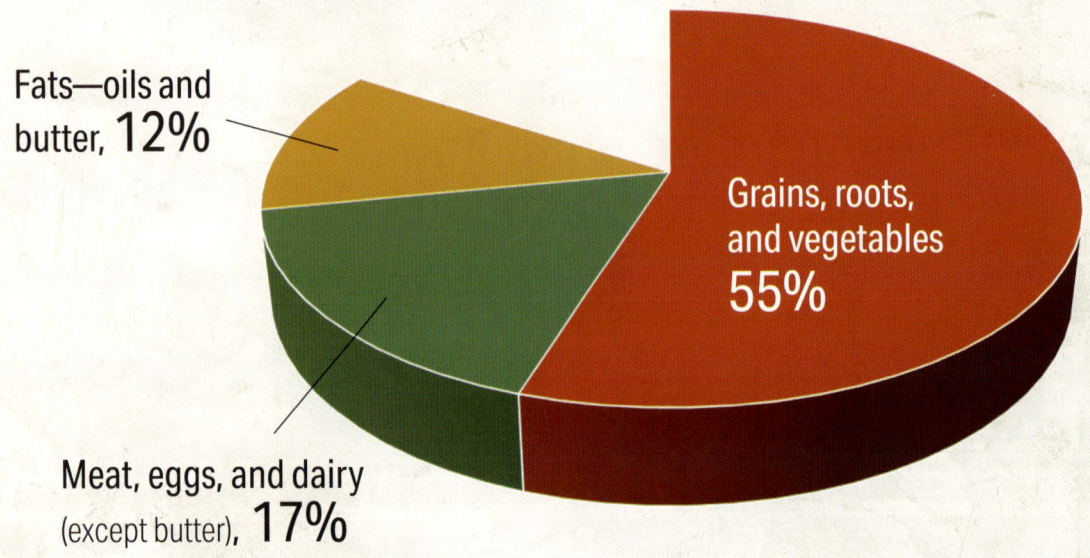

Fats—oils and butter, 12%

Grains, roots, and vegetables 55%

Meat, eggs, and dairy (except butter), 17%

Twelve percent of the calories would come from fats and oils, and these would be used by most of the villagers in some way. Butter is rare in many countries, but most people use some kind of oil when preparing their food.

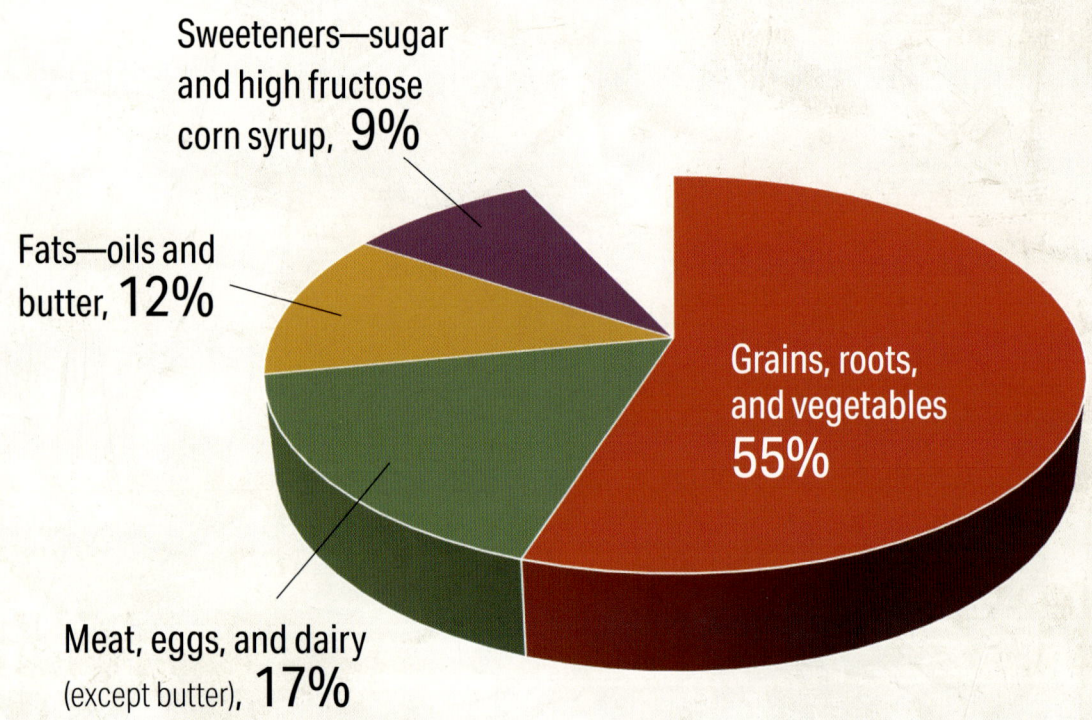

Sweeteners—sugar and high fructose corn syrup, **9%**

Fats—oils and butter, **12%**

Grains, roots, and vegetables **55%**

Meat, eggs, and dairy (except butter), **17%**

Various kinds of sweeteners would provide about 9% of the calories consumed in the village.

Many kinds of soda and other sugary drinks provide a large percentage of this. Soft drinks have found their way into extremely poor countries.

In 2023, Coca-Cola could be purchased in every country except North Korea and Cuba, where trade embargoes and sanctions have been in place for many years.[1] So almost everyone in your village would be familiar with Coke.

---

[1] The embargo on North Korea was enacted in 1950 and in Cuba in 1962.

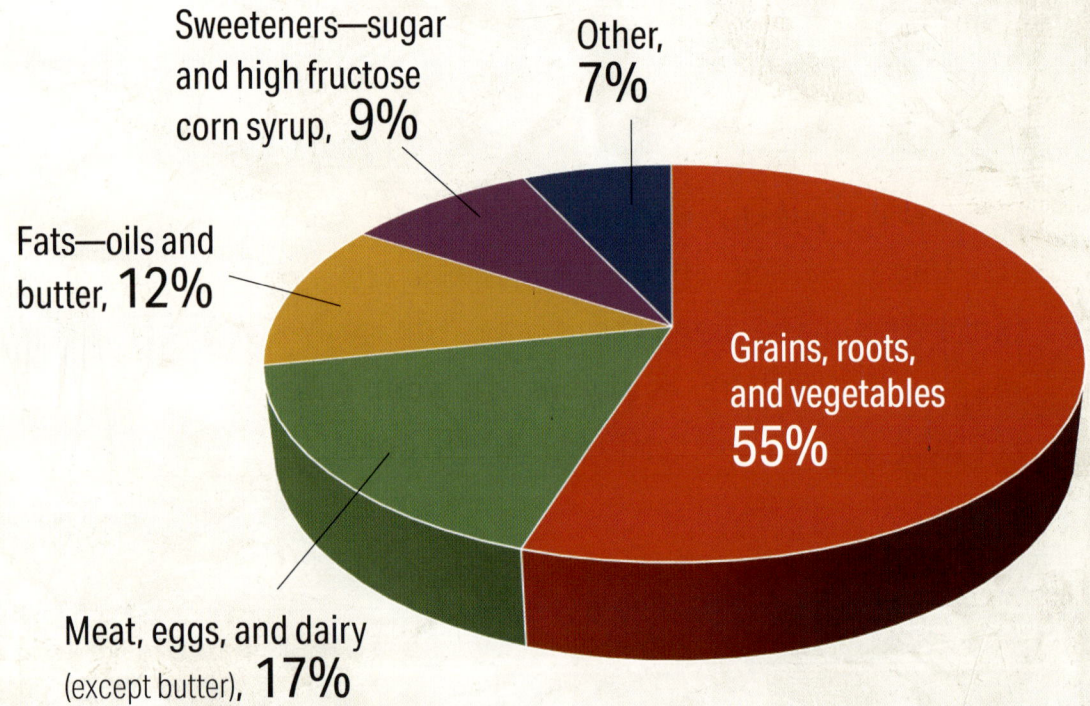

Sweeteners—sugar and high fructose corn syrup, 9%

Other, 7%

Fats—oils and butter, 12%

Grains, roots, and vegetables 55%

Meat, eggs, and dairy (except butter), 17%

The other 7% of the calories includes alcoholic beverages and other foods not readily categorized into the other groups.

The cost of the food is another difference you would observe in your village. The people from wealthier countries see food as a fairly minor expense, but for many of the others, food can be a major percentage of their income. Let's compare a few countries.

Household Income
Spent on Food

In America, food only requires about **11%** of the average family budget, and roughly half of this is spent on eating out.

Food
11%

Other 89%

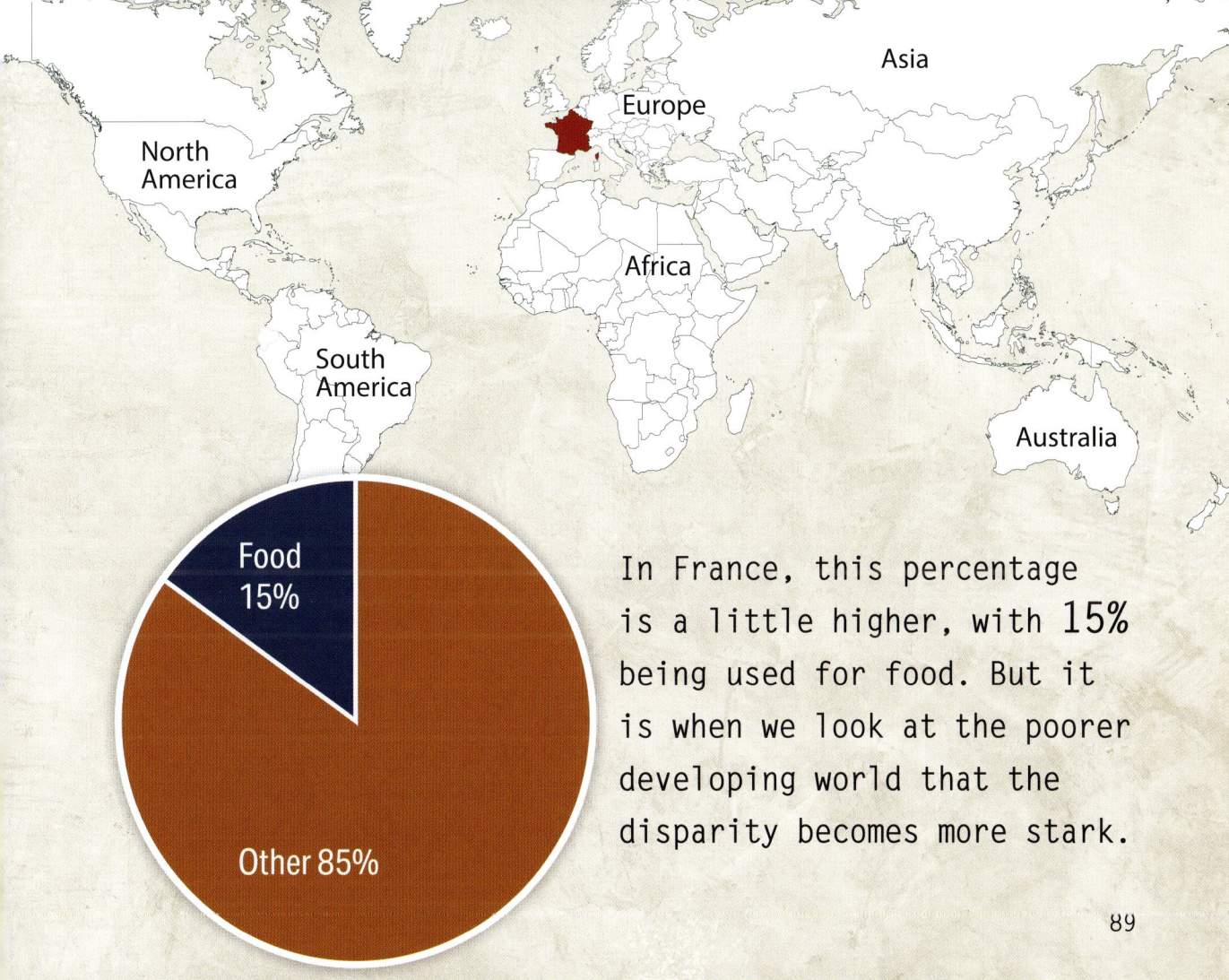

North America

South America

Europe

Asia

Africa

Australia

Food 15%

Other 85%

In France, this percentage is a little higher, with 15% being used for food. But it is when we look at the poorer developing world that the disparity becomes more stark.

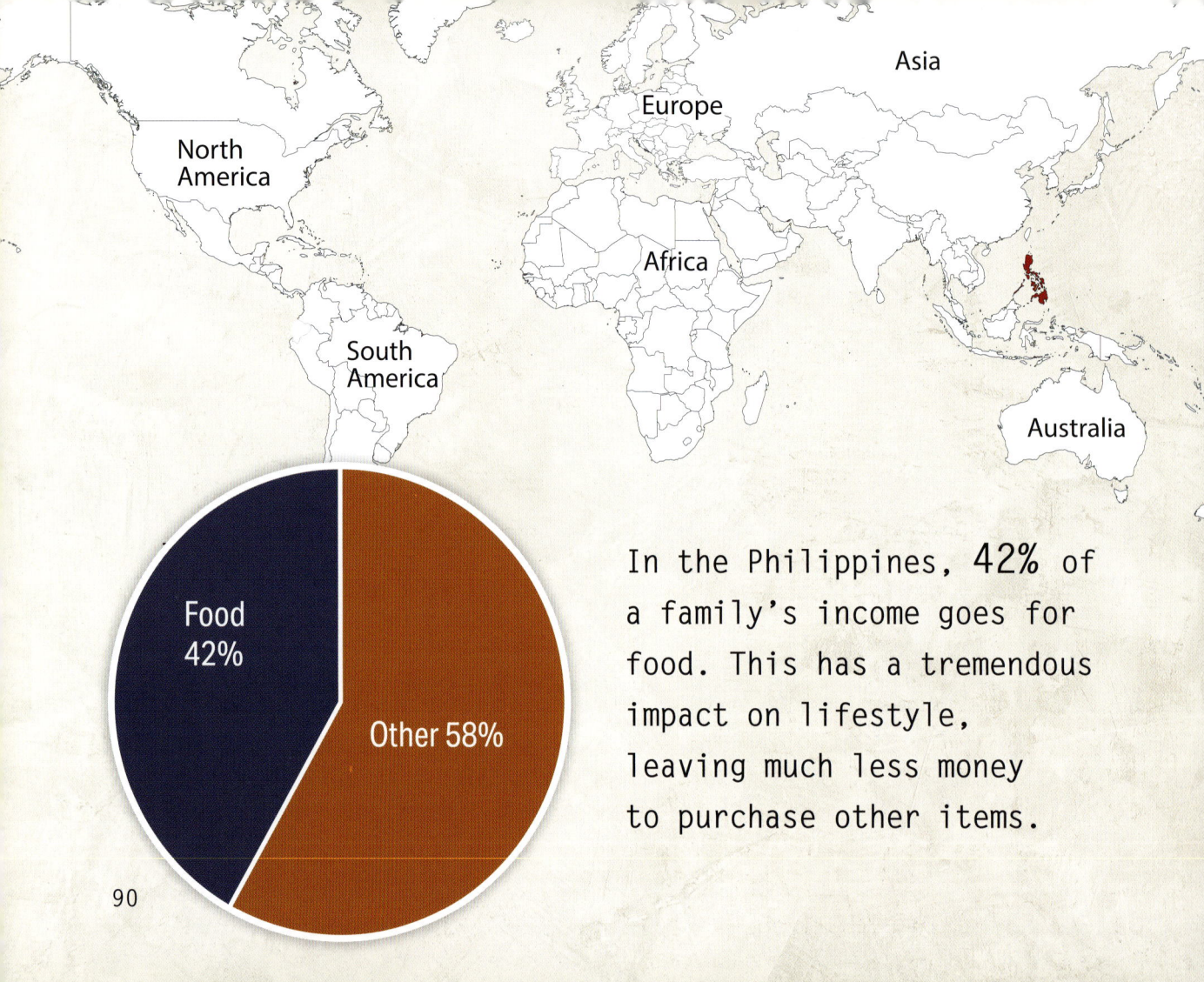

North America

South America

Europe

Asia

Africa

Australia

Food 42%

Other 58%

In the Philippines, **42%** of a family's income goes for food. This has a tremendous impact on lifestyle, leaving much less money to purchase other items.

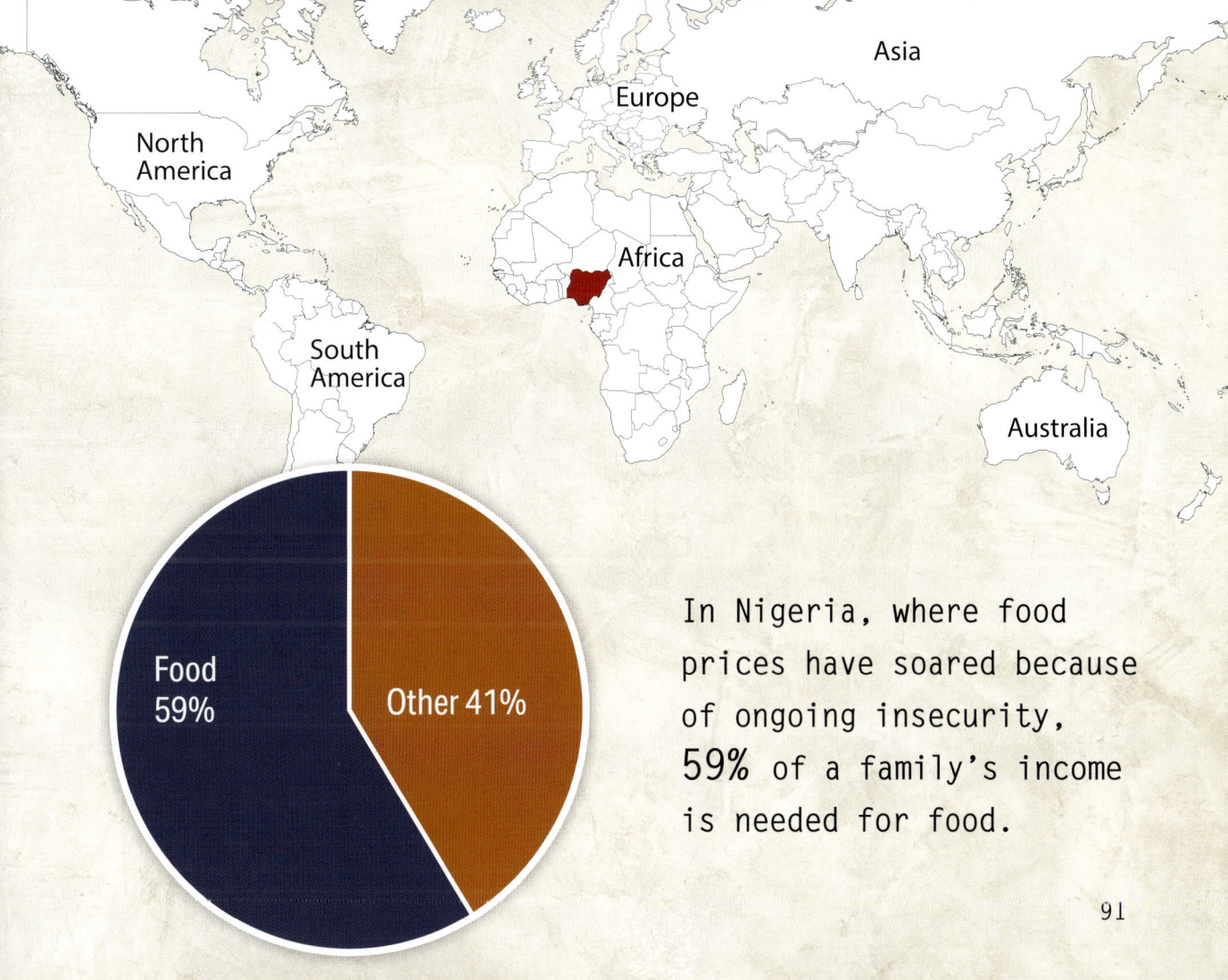

North America

South America

Europe

Asia

Africa

Australia

Food 59%

Other 41%

In Nigeria, where food prices have soared because of ongoing insecurity, **59%** of a family's income is needed for food.

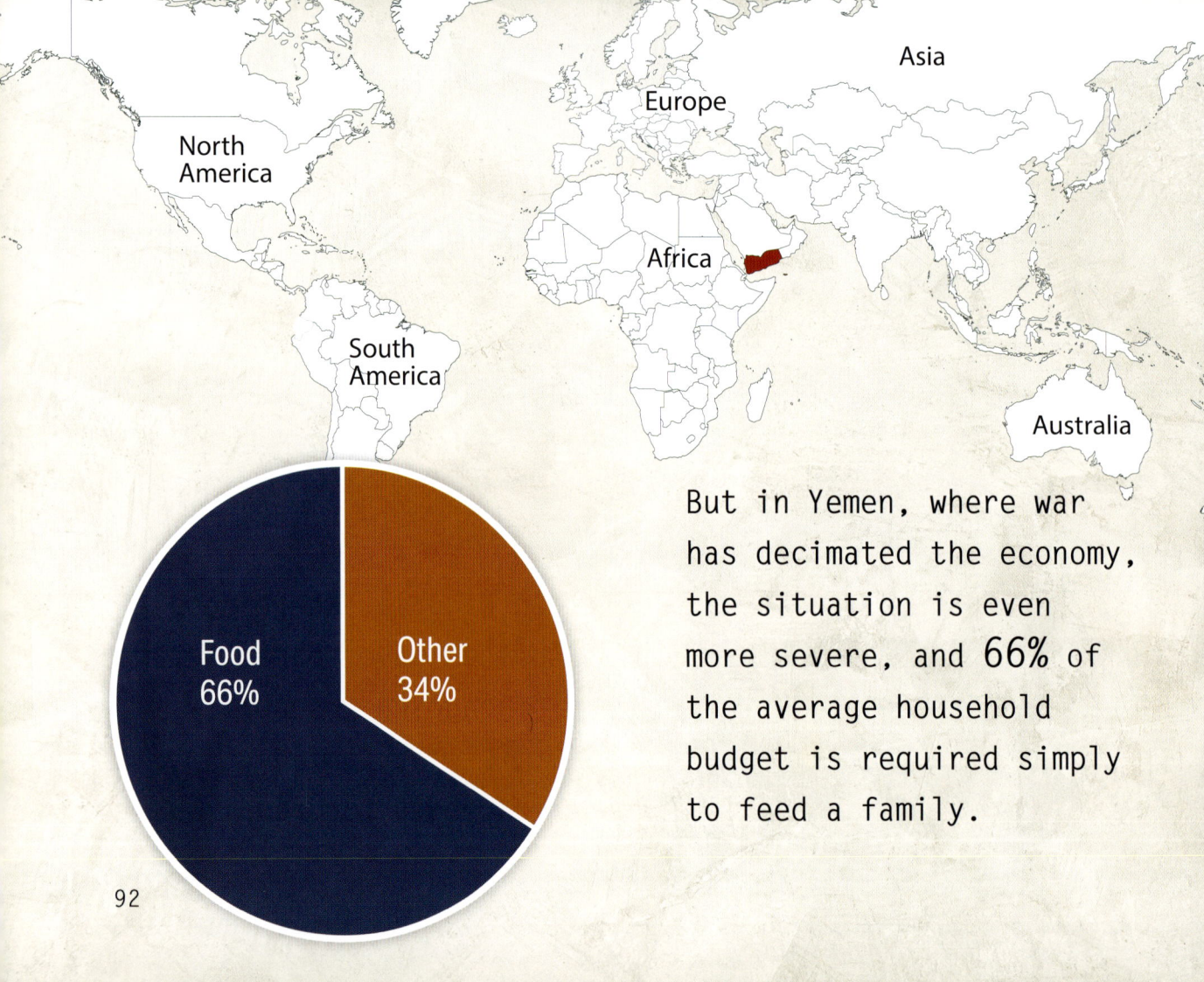

North
America

South
America

Europe

Asia

Africa

Australia

Food
66%

Other
34%

But in Yemen, where war
has decimated the economy,
the situation is even
more severe, and **66%** of
the average household
budget is required simply
to feed a family.

And remember, these are averages.
This means that the extremely poor are
spending an even higher percentage
on food as they struggle to survive.

America
France
Philippines
Nigeria
Yemen

66
59
42
15
11

So in your village there would
be a big variation. Some of your
neighbors would have difficulty
finding enough money to purchase
food, while others would give
prices very little thought.

One of the reasons it is difficult to
get a good grasp on global nutrition is
because we are constantly bombarded with
conflicting and confusing statistics.

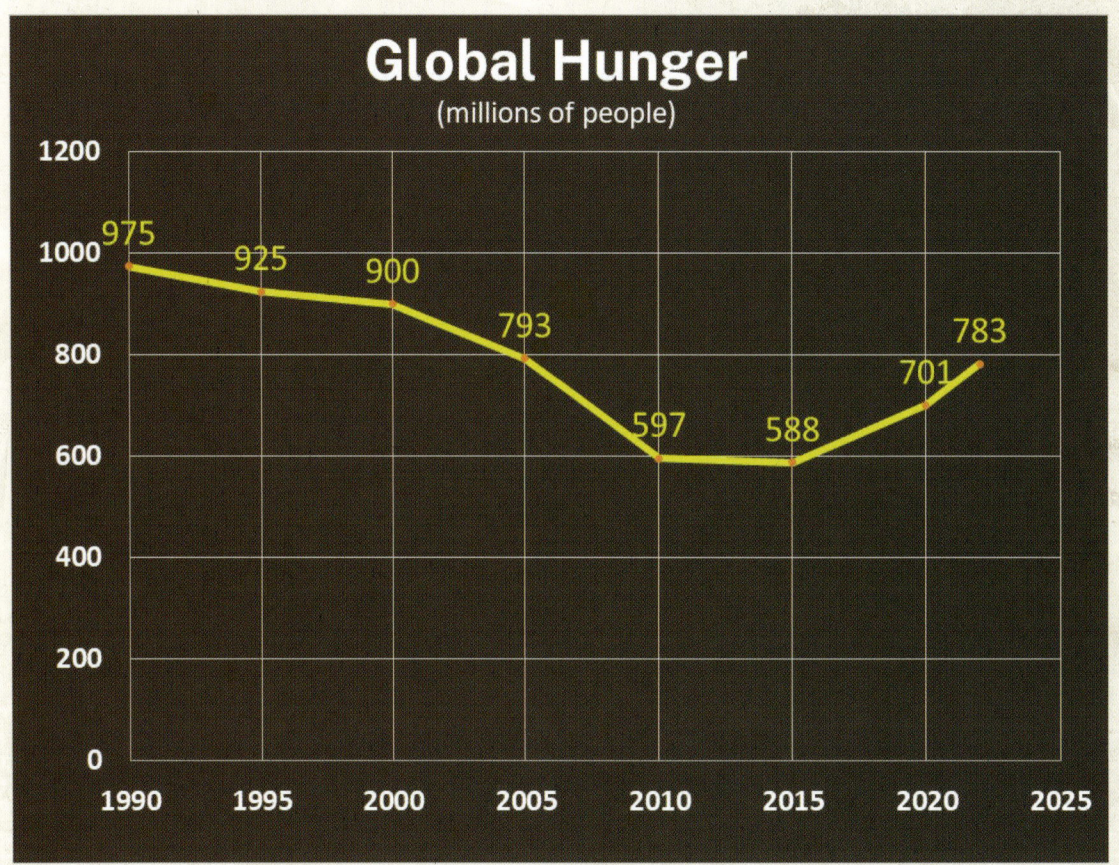

Global Hunger
(millions of people)

For years, global hunger decreased.
As larger countries like China and
India prospered, incomes grew and
food became more plentiful. But in the
past 10 years, the number of hungry
people in the world has been growing.

HUNGER

- Globally, almost 800 million people are hungry.

- 3 million children die each year from malnutrition.

- A child dies from hunger every 10 seconds.

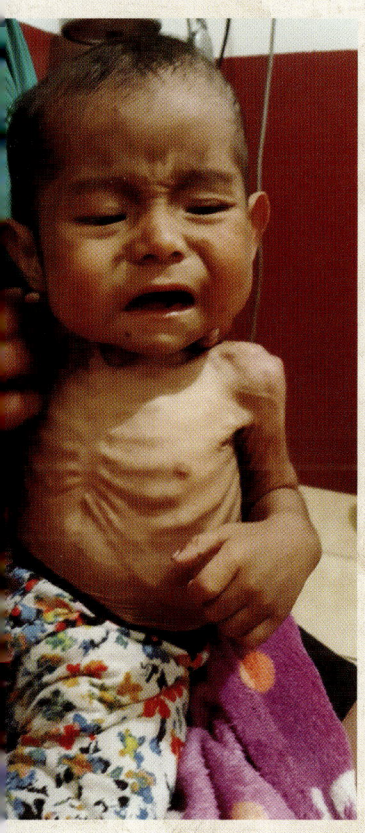

Statistics like these make us stop
and think. This means that every
15 minutes, 90 children die from a
lack of food. These numbers can be
misleading since they include children
dying of diseases resulting from an
inadequate immune system caused by
poor malnutrition. But any way we look
at it, these are sobering numbers!
 But some other numbers
are also growing...

OBESITY

- 2.8 million people die each year from obesity.

- Globally, more are overweight than underweight.

- It is estimated that by 2035, half of the people in the world will be obese.

Obesity is a huge problem as well!
So what is going on? How can both
obesity and hunger be growing?
 To get a better picture, let's return
to our village of 100. What would
nutrition look like in our village?
 Let's start with those who are
struggling to survive.

Regularly experience hunger.

10

Ten people would regularly experience hunger. They have insufficient calorie intake and are malnourished.

Regularly experience hunger.

Not always sure where their next meal is coming from.

20

Another 20 people are not always sure where their next meal is coming from. They are part of the 2.4 billion people who are either moderately or severely food insecure.

Regularly experience hunger.

Not always sure where their next meal is coming from.

Have access to good food and a well balanced diet

31

Thirty-one villagers would have access to good food and a well-balanced diet.

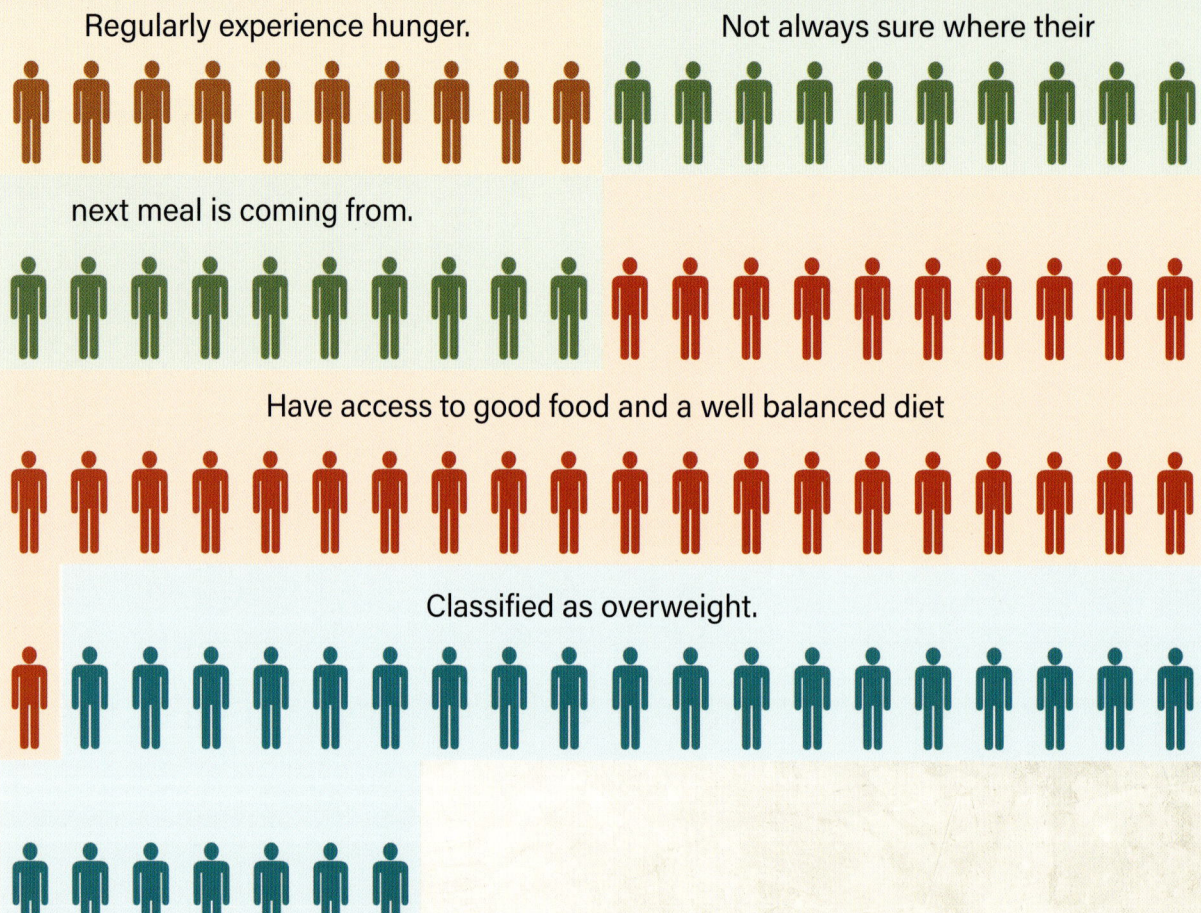

Regularly experience hunger.

Not always sure where their next meal is coming from.

Have access to good food and a well balanced diet

Classified as overweight.

26

Twenty-six would be classified as overweight.
They have access to plenty of food and
are consuming more than they need.

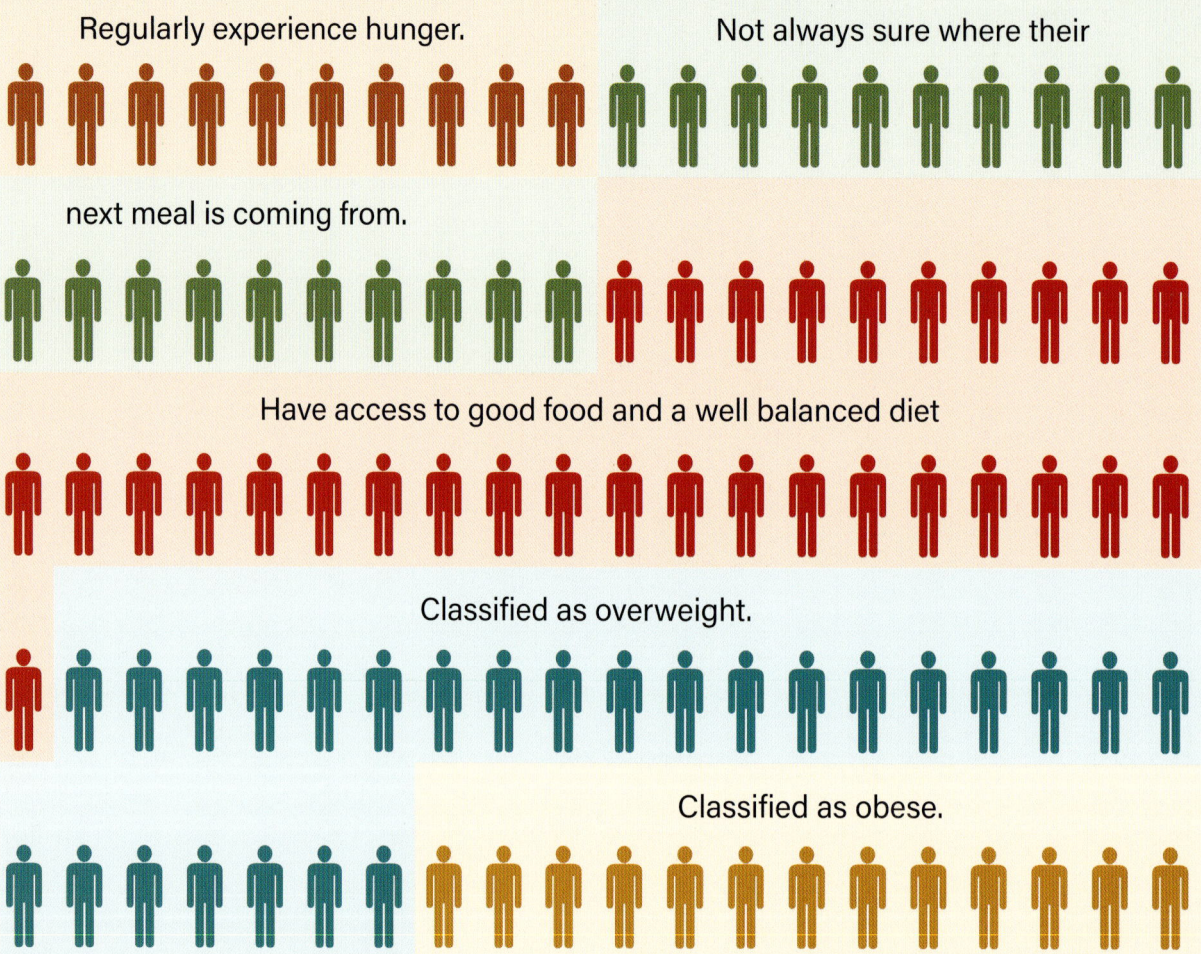

Regularly experience hunger.

Not always sure where their

next meal is coming from.

Have access to good food and a well balanced diet

Classified as overweight.

Classified as obese.

13

Finally, 13 villagers would be obese.
To be classified as obese, a man must
be approximately 100 pounds overweight
and a woman 80 pounds overweight.

This means **30** villagers would not
be receiving sufficient nutrition,
but **39** others would be consuming
more than they need. Ironically,
both obesity and hunger would
be increasing in your village.
  So let's look closer.

The problem is not a lack of food—our world produces plenty! If food were distributed evenly, it is estimated that each person, even the children, would have almost 3,000 calories a day. In fact, it is estimated that 10 billion people could live comfortably on the food currently produced!

But consumption of calories isn't distributed evenly, and food consumption varies greatly depending on where you live.

Let's look at this disparity across five countries.

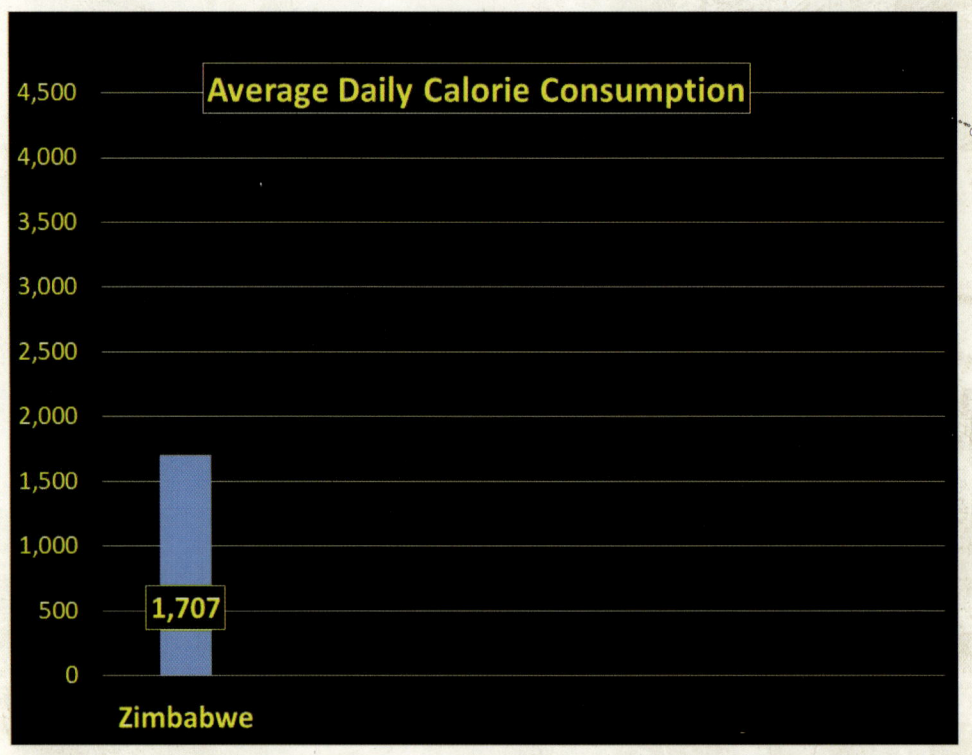

In Zimbabwe, located in southern Africa, the average citizen consumes under 2,000 calories per day. This varies from year to year, depending on the economy and the weather. Maize and wheat are major staples, so when there is a lack of rainfall, food can be scarce.

117

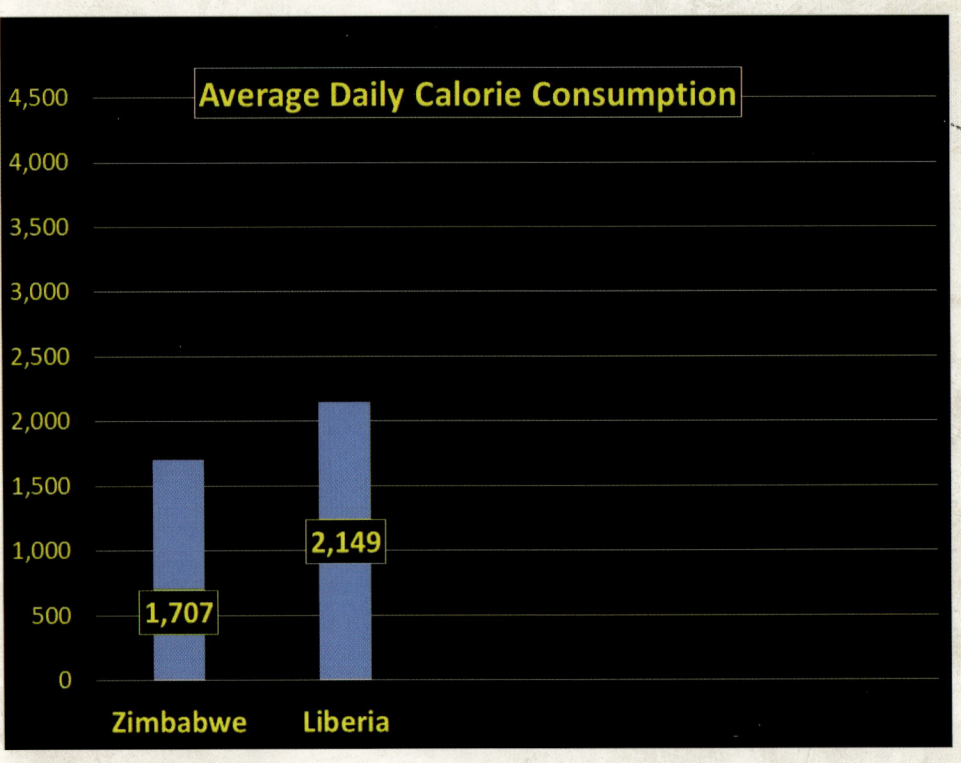

Asia

Europe

Africa

South
America

Australia

In Liberia, on the west side of
Africa, people enjoy more rainfall and a
little better diet. Rice and various root
vegetables are common, and the average
calorie consumption is over 2,000.

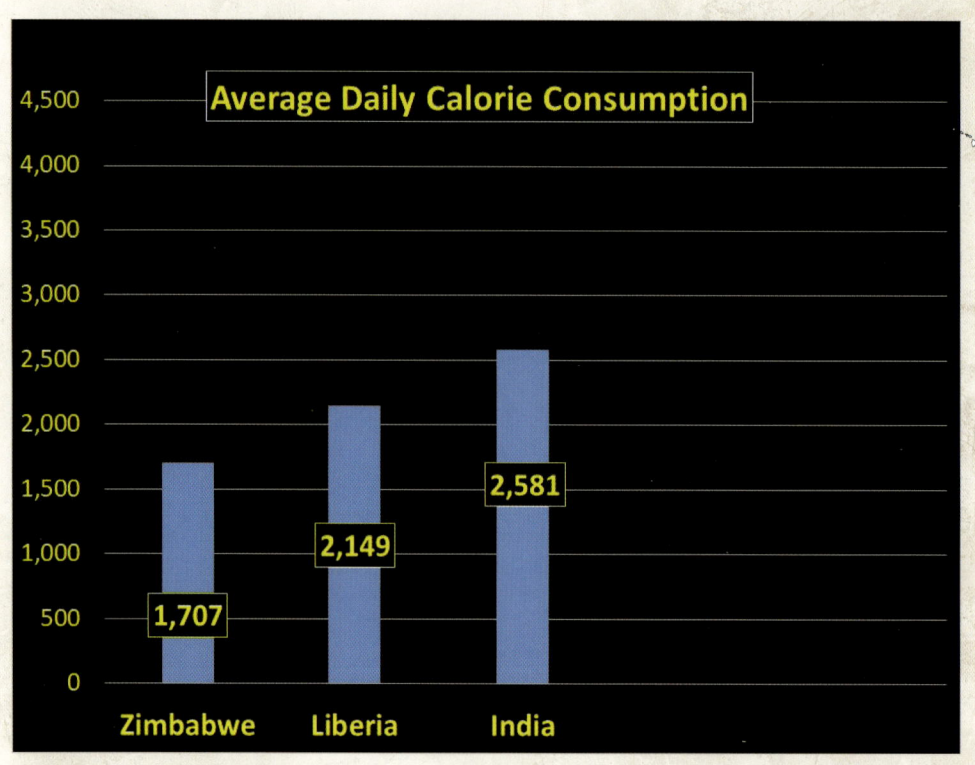

Asia

Europe

Africa

South
America

Australia

India has a wide variety of
foods, with the national average
calorie consumption over 2,500.

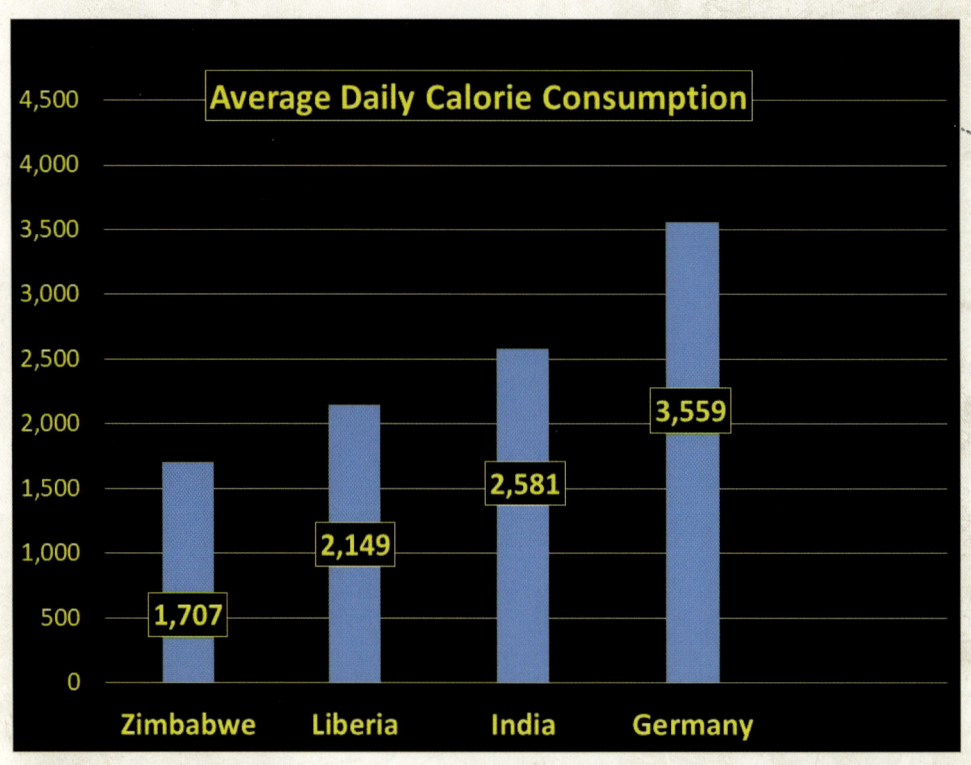

People living in Western Europe have a much better diet, with access to a wide variety of nutritious foods. The average **German** consumes more than twice the calories of countries like Zimbabwe.

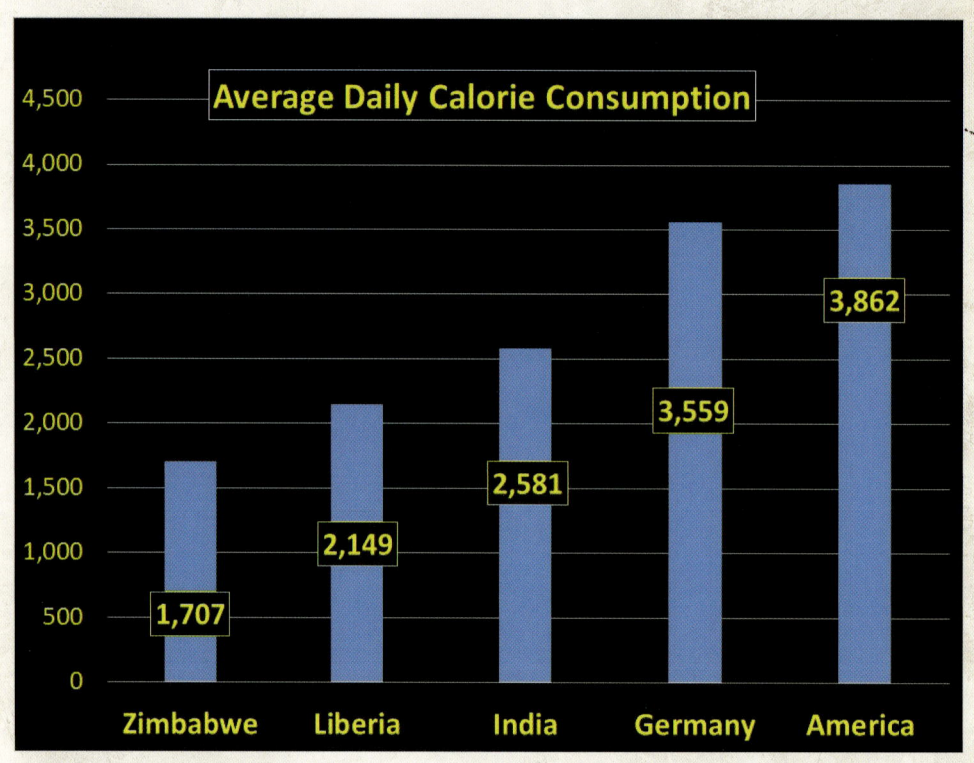

And finally, the **United States**. The average American citizen consumes over 3,800 calories each day, with a diet heavy in meat, sugar, and fats. In addition, Americans tend to eat much larger portions than those in other countries.

WHY DO A FEW HAVE SO MUCH, WHILE SO MANY HAVE SO LITTLE?

As we have seen, some have too little and others have too much. And strangely, those who eat the most spend a much smaller percentage of their budget doing it.

So what is God seeing, and what should those of us who have so much be doing?

Before answering this question, let's back up and consider another one. If there is plenty of food, why are millions hungry?

Let's take a closer look at the root causes of hunger in our world.

Root Causes of
World Hunger

- WAR—starvation as a military weapon

Conflict is a major cause of hunger and
malnutrition. Evil men use their power to
restrict the production and flow of needed
resources. The goal is to starve the
opposing population into submission. We see
examples of this in Ethiopia, Yemen, Syria,
and other places where food shortages
are man-made and used as a weapon.

Root Causes of
World Hunger

- WAR—starvation as a military weapon
- GREED & CORRUPTION—oppressive systems

Around the globe, there are many places where the wealthy oppress the poor. Insufficient wages, unethical money lending, and even human slavery are major problems. Many people cannot earn enough to provide adequate food and clothing for their families. This is driven by human greed. Systems are purposefully designed to keep the materially poor from owning property or advancing financially. Corrupt governments and oppressive business schemes are major contributors to global hunger.

Root Causes of
World Hunger

- WAR—starvation as a military weapon
- GREED & CORRUPTION—oppressive systems
- POVERTY—food available but too expensive

In many countries plenty of food exists, but for a variety of reasons it remains out of reach of the poorest. Sometimes high prices are weather related, but more often the problem is man-made.

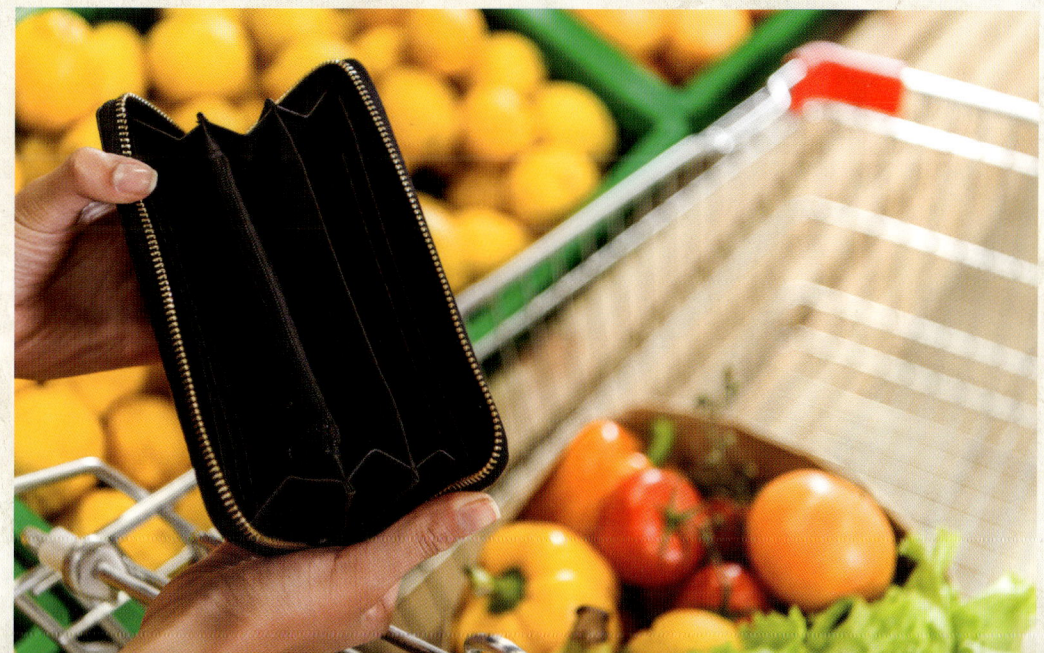

Root Causes of
World Hunger

- WAR—starvation as a military weapon
- GREED & CORRUPTION—oppressive systems
- POVERTY—food available but too expensive
- DISCRIMINATION—ethnic prejudice

Racism continues to contribute to hunger. In India, the caste you are born into can have a huge impact on what your dinner plate looks like. In places like Brazil, some indigenous communities are marginalized and experience malnutrition simply because of their ethnicity.

Root Causes of
World Hunger

- WAR—starvation as a military weapon
- GREED & CORRUPTION—oppressive systems
- POVERTY—food available but too expensive
- DISCRIMINATION—ethnic prejudice
- IGNORANCE—lack of management skills

There is a major need for agricultural teaching in many of the poorest countries where the world's hungriest people live. Though there may be great potential, their resources are not being utilized well. Sometimes what is harvested is lost because of poor storage practices. Many times this is due to a worldview that discourages innovation and makes new methods appear futile.

Root Causes of
World Hunger

- WAR—starvation as a military weapon
- GREED & CORRUPTION—oppressive systems
- POVERTY—food available but too expensive
- DISCRIMINATION—ethnic prejudice
- IGNORANCE—lack of management skills
- INEQUITY—rich consuming more than needed

Finally, inequity exists because the rich consume more than they need. Americans consume an estimated 815 billion calories of food each day, roughly 200 billion more than needed. It has been estimated that America's excess alone would be enough to feed 80 million people. How should American Christians respond to this global disparity?

Maybe it is time for us to go back and see what the Bible says about consuming more than we need. The Bible calls it gluttony, but here in America, where "bigger is better," we tend to forget.

"But the days will come, when the bridegroom shall be taken from them, and then shall they fast." Matthew 9:15

"Be not among winebibbers; among riotous eaters of flesh: for the drunkard and the glutton shall come to poverty." Proverbs 23:20-21

"All things are lawful unto me, but all things are not expedient: all things are lawful for me, but I will not be brought under the power of any." 1 Corinthians 6:12

"Behold, this was the iniquity of thy sister Sodom, pride, fulness of bread, and abundance of idleness was in her and in her daughters, neither did she strengthen the hand of the poor and needy." Ezekiel 16:49

"Whether therefore ye eat, or drink, or whatsoever ye do, do all to the glory of God." 1 Corinthians 10:31

"Whose end is destruction, whose God is their belly…" Philippians 3:19

Drunkenness and adultery are evils we take very seriously. Yet gluttony, a sin closely linked in Scripture to these sins, is one we tend to minimize, laugh about, and even accept as harmless. It has become so common in America that we rarely give it much thought. But the Bible repeatedly refers to the sin of gluttony. Christians should be known for disciplined lifestyles rather than overindulgence—for fasting rather than continual feasting.

  So what is the solution for world hunger? Let's try to imagine what that world could look like.

Solution for World Hunger?

- Peace—turn swords into plowshares

Visualize a world where each person learned to love one's enemies and where there were no wars. Where starvation was not used as a weapon and where all the energy and ingenuity that currently goes into killing was used to develop solutions to global poverty and fiscal disparity. What kind of world would that be?

Solution for World Hunger?

- Peace—turn swords into plowshares
- Love—treat others as we would be treated

What if people around the globe would start sharing, loving, and treating each other as Jesus instructed? Imagine what this might look like! This would surely move us much closer to a hunger-free world.

Solution for World Hunger?

- Peace—turn swords into plowshares
- Love—treat others as we would be treated
- Equity—no respect of persons

Imagine a world of equity! Where all people are valued, not because of the country they were born in, their financial assets, or their skin color, but because they are made in the image of God. God wants all of His children to flourish, regardless of who and where they are. Understanding this truth would make our world much more beautiful!

Solution for World Hunger?

- Peace—turn swords into plowshares
- Love—treat others as we would be treated
- Equity—no respect of persons
- Biblical teaching—Christian worldview

There is a tremendous need for Biblical teaching in our world. As Hosea said long ago:

"My people are destroyed for lack of knowledge."

Hosea 4:6

Growing up with the Bible shapes our worldview. In Genesis, we learn who created the earth and how God intends for us to care for it. The book of Proverbs teaches us cause and effect, the importance of a good work ethic, and the value of saving and planning for the future.

The Old Law taught Israel good
sanitation and personal hygiene,
something that many parts of our world
still need to be taught. All of this is
important as we interact with the material
world and provide food for our families.

If the entire world had a Biblical
worldview, it would have a huge
impact on health and nutrition.

Solution for World Hunger?

- Peace—turn swords into plowshares
- Love—treat others as we would be treated
- Equity—no respect of persons
- Biblical teaching—Christian worldview
- Individual lives transformed by Jesus

The greatest need today isn't better social programs, better laws, or getting the right people into power. Rather, healthy communities develop when individuals gain a Biblical worldview and are transformed by the saving power of Jesus. While our world will not experience a complete renovation before Jesus returns, we can see little glimpses of this reality in the lives of transformed people.

What does following Jesus have to do with alleviating world hunger? When the Holy Spirit arrives in a man's life, his focus turns outward, and he will immediately begin to care for and share with others.

In the early church, we don't read that they were commanded to distribute their goods—it just happened! And as each person shared, a beautiful representation of the kingdom of God was exhibited in a powerful way.

Just as Jesus fed the hungry, so transformed
lives will help feed people in our day.

While visiting the Rohingya refugee camp in Bangladesh, I interviewed this 9-year-old girl named Asma. She is holding her brother, and her grandfather is standing behind her. When asked what her favorite food was, she said beef. She almost never had any beef to eat, but it wasn't that it was unavailable in the camp. In their culture, men are entitled to the best food, so whenever they had beef, her father and grandfather ate as much as they wanted. And by the time they were finished, there wasn't any left for the children.

Don't underestimate the importance
of worldview. The transforming
power of Jesus would not only change
this grandfather's life, it would
also provide beef for the children!

Solution for World Hunger?

- Peace—turn swords into plowshares
- Love—treat others as we would be treated
- Equity—no respect of persons
- Biblical teaching—Christian worldview
- Individual lives transformed by Jesus
- Church communities demonstrating Jubilee

Finally, imagine church communities scattered over the entire globe collectively demonstrating love, peace, equity, and sacrificial commitment for others. These would be church communities like we read about in the book of Acts, where people have been transformed by Jesus and now care about and share with others.

The solution for world hunger is actually spiritual revival—a change of heart in which church communities with a Jesus worldview are working together. This is why Jesus didn't come to reform the existing kingdoms of this world—He came to proclaim an entirely new kingdom! Jesus called this the kingdom of God.

The solution to our global hunger is having a world that honors Jesus as King! And while we do not expect hunger to be completely alleviated until Jesus returns, we have the opportunity to demonstrate a credible representation of God's kingdom in our local churches. We can create little communities where unbelievers can see the hungry being fed, the naked being clothed, and the lonely finding a place of belonging.

The Kingdom of God

We are living in a world of opportunity! Let us continue to reach out and demonstrate the kingdom that Jesus proclaimed. Let us keep sharing, teaching, and exhibiting sacrificial love in our local church communities.

Advancing the kingdom
of God is the ultimate
solution for world hunger!

About the Author

Gary Miller was raised in California and today lives with his wife Patty and family in the Pacific Northwest. Gary works with the poor in developing countries and directs the SALT Microfinance Solutions program for Christian Aid Ministries. This program offers business and spiritual teaching to those living in chronic poverty. It provides small loans, sets up local village savings groups, and assists them in learning how to use their God-given resources to become sustainable.

Gary has authored numerous books on kingdom living, several booklets for outreach purposes, and some microfinance manuals.

Have you been inspired by Gary's materials? Maybe you have questions, or perhaps you even disagree with the author. Share your thoughts by sending an email to kingdomfinance@camoh.org or writing to Christian Aid Ministries, P.O. Box 360, Berlin, Ohio 44610.